The Declutteri

Simple Steps to Clear Space, ~~Reduce~~ Simplify Your Life for Good

By Amelia Walsh

About the Author

Amelia Walsh is a British author who specialises in helping women simplify their homes, minds, and lives. With a background in psychology and a personal journey through overwhelm and emotional burnout, she writes with gentle honesty and practical insight.

Amelia lives in the English countryside with her daughter, where a house move two years ago prompted her own powerful decluttering reset—one that revealed the emotional weight hidden in everyday possessions and the freedom that comes with letting go.

She is passionate about helping readers create space for what truly matters, develop kinder habits, and build calm routines that last. Her work blends mindset, home organisation, and emotional wellbeing to support real, lasting change—without the pressure of perfection.

The Decluttering Reset is her heartfelt invitation to anyone ready to clear space, reduce stress, and start living more intentionally, one small step at a time.

Introduction: What Is a Decluttering Reset?

Most of us don't realise how much clutter we carry—until we start to clear it. It's not just the piles on the kitchen counter or the overstuffed drawers we swear we'll deal with "next weekend." It's the mental noise, the weight of decisions postponed, and the unspoken guilt of holding on to things we no longer need but don't know how to let go of.

Decluttering isn't just about getting rid of things. It's about **resetting**—your space, your habits, your stress levels, and even your mindset. That's what this book is here to help you do. Whether you're overwhelmed by your home, drowning in digital distractions, or just craving some breathing room, *The Decluttering Reset* offers a fresh and achievable way forward.

A Personal Turning Point

Two years ago, an important life event forced me to do what I'd been avoiding: we moved house. Like many people, I assumed I was reasonably organised. But the moment I had to start packing, the reality hit me—**we had accumulated far more than we ever needed**, used, or even liked. Every cupboard, drawer, and attic box was packed with forgotten, unfinished, or sentimental things. It was overwhelming.

But here's what surprised me: once I let go of all the excess, **the benefits were enormous**. Our new space felt calmer. My mind felt clearer. Everyday life became lighter. It wasn't just the house that changed—it was my whole way of thinking. I had more time, more focus, and more energy for what actually mattered.

In **Chapter 5**, I'll show you how to approach each room practically and without stress. In **Chapter 10**, we'll explore simple systems that keep your home clear long after a big clean-out—and how you can avoid sliding back into chaos.

Clutter Is Personal

One of the reasons decluttering feels so hard is because **clutter is deeply personal**. For me, I'm what you'll discover in Chapter 2 is called a *Sentimental Saver*. I'd kept nearly everything my daughter ever made or wrote at school—from scribbled stories to glittery art projects held together by hope and glue. These things feel like memories, proof of our journey together. Letting go can feel like losing part of that.

But what I've learned is this: **keeping everything can actually bury the memories** we value most. When everything is saved, nothing stands out. By choosing what to keep more intentionally, we give the most special items room to shine.

You'll find a **Clutter Personality Quiz in Chapter 2** to help you discover your own type—whether you're a Sentimental Saver like me, a Just-in-Case Hoarder, or someone who avoids decluttering altogether. This insight will help you approach the rest of the reset in a way that works *with* your personality, not against it.

The Reset Mindset

This book is about *resetting*, not reaching perfection. You don't need a minimalist home worthy of a magazine. You just need to create enough space—for peace, for clarity, for life to feel a little lighter. You'll learn how to:

- Let go of things with less guilt (see Chapter 4)

- Clear space room by room without feeling overwhelmed (see Chapter 5)

- Declutter your mind, time, and digital world—not just your cupboards (see Chapters 6 and 7)

- Create simple, sustainable habits that stop the clutter from coming back (see Chapter 10)

As you move through this book, you'll find practical tips, mindset shifts, and gentle encouragement to guide your journey. And when you're ready to put it all into action, Chapter 12 includes a special bonus: the **21-Day Decluttering Reset Challenge**. This simple, structured plan is designed to help you build momentum and stay on track—one small, manageable step at a time. Whether you follow it now or return to it later, it's there to support you whenever life starts to feel cluttered again.

To help you stay grounded and gently integrate what you've read, you'll also find a **Reset Ritual** at the end of every chapter. These short, calming practices offer a moment of reflection, intention, or action—designed to reinforce your progress and reconnect you with your "why." Whether it's a simple journal prompt, a mindful pause, or a one-minute task, each ritual gives you a practical next step that brings clarity and momentum without overwhelm. Think of them as your reset buttons—there whenever you need to come back to calm.

By the end, you'll feel more than just tidy—you'll feel **reset**. Ready to live with less stress, fewer distractions, and more of what truly matters.

So let's begin. Gently, step by step. You don't need to rush. You just need to start.

Chapter 1: The Hidden Burden of Clutter

Clutter isn't just a mess on your floor or an overflowing drawer—it's an invisible weight many of us carry every single day. It piles up in corners, closets, inboxes, calendars, and, perhaps most heavily, in our minds. While we might joke about "the junk drawer" or the spare room we'd rather not open, the truth is that clutter affects us far more deeply than we realise.

If you've ever walked into a room and instantly felt your shoulders tighten...
If you've struggled to focus because your environment feels chaotic...
If you've found yourself snapping at loved ones or procrastinating, only to realise the mess around you is fuelling your anxiety...
You already know: **clutter is more than physical**. It's emotional. It's mental. It's exhausting.

When Clutter Feels Like Control

Many of us don't notice clutter creeping in. It builds slowly, almost silently. A few extra mugs you never use, the unopened post on the hallway table, the pair of shoes that never get put away but you tell yourself you might wear one day. At first, it seems harmless.

In fact, sometimes we keep things because it gives us a *false sense of control*. "If I just had better storage, I'd feel organised," we tell ourselves. Or "I'll use that eventually, so I should keep it just in case." But clutter isn't the result of a lack of space or containers—it's often the result of *deferred decisions*. Every item we delay dealing with becomes another unanswered question quietly asking, "What are you going to do with me?"

The Mental Load of Clutter

Clutter demands attention, even when we're not actively dealing with it. It pulls at our focus. It adds to the background noise of our lives. Researchers have found that living in cluttered environments increases levels of the stress hormone cortisol. That means even if you're not aware of it, your nervous system is responding— heightened, tense, overloaded.

A cluttered environment also contributes to:

- **Decision fatigue**: Too much visual noise wears out your brain faster.

- **Decreased productivity**: You're more easily distracted and less efficient.

- **Poor sleep**: Bedrooms full of clutter can lead to increased anxiety and restlessness.

- **Relationship tension**: Shared spaces that feel out of control often spark arguments.

The point is: clutter doesn't just stay in the room—it travels with you. Into your mood, your thoughts, and your energy.

When I Realised It Was Too Much

When I moved house two years ago with my daughter, I was forced to face the reality of just how much I'd been holding on to. At the time, I considered myself fairly tidy—I didn't think of my home as "cluttered." But the minute I had to put everything into boxes, I was stunned.

There were cupboards I hadn't opened in years, full of things I didn't even remember owning. There were boxes labelled "important" that hadn't been touched since the last move. And then there were the sentimental items—so many of them. I'd kept almost everything my daughter had ever made or written at school. Tiny art projects, notebooks filled with doodles, handwritten cards, spelling tests with gold stars. All of it felt precious. And some of it still is.

But somewhere in the process of sorting, I had a realisation: **I was drowning in memory clutter.** And more than that, I was overwhelmed by the guilt of letting anything go.

That move became the beginning of my reset—not just of my space, but of how I relate to things. I saw the way clutter had crept into my life, quietly but relentlessly. I saw how it had become a barrier to clarity, not a comfort.

What Clutter Isn't

It's important to pause here and say: *decluttering is not about shame or minimalism extremes.*
This book is not going to ask you to live out of a suitcase or count how many socks you own. You don't need to be ruthless. You just need to be honest.

Clutter is not:

- A sign that you're lazy

- Something you should feel embarrassed about

- A reflection of your worth or intelligence

Life is busy. Emotions are complicated. Stuff accumulates. That's all normal. But if you're reading this book, it likely means you're ready to make a change—not just to your home, but to how you *feel* in it.

What Decluttering Really Does

When you reset your space, something surprising happens: **your thoughts begin to settle too**. The corners of your mind that felt noisy and chaotic begin to quiet down. You stop feeling so reactive. You breathe a little deeper. You focus a little better.

Here are just a few of the benefits you can expect as you begin your reset:

1. **Increased mental clarity** – Less visual noise means more focus.

2. **Reduced stress and anxiety** – You'll stop feeling so "on edge" at home.

3. **Improved relationships** – Calm spaces foster more patience and connection.

4. **Better time management** – You'll spend less time looking for things or cleaning up.

5. **More intentional living** – With fewer distractions, you'll do more of what matters.

6. **Greater self-trust** – Each decision to let go builds confidence and calm.

The beauty of decluttering is that it doesn't require a huge life overhaul. Just small, honest steps—one at a time.

Clutter and Emotion: The Deeper Link

Clutter is rarely just about the stuff. More often, it's about the *story* behind the stuff.

- That pile of magazines? A reminder of the hobbies you meant to start.

- Those jeans you haven't worn in years? A symbol of who you used to be—or who you hope to become.

- That drawer full of cables and chargers? A refusal to waste or let go, just in case.

And then there's the sentimental clutter—the hardest kind to deal with. Like I mentioned earlier, I'm what you'll discover in Chapter 2 is called a *Sentimental Saver*. I find it incredibly hard to part with anything tied to a memory, especially when it relates to my daughter. Her childhood feels like it flew by, and each tiny item feels like a fragile piece of it I'm afraid to lose.

But here's what I've learned: **memories are not in the object.** They're in *you*. You can keep the most meaningful pieces without keeping everything. In fact, by curating what you keep, you give those memories the honour they deserve.

What This Book Will Help You Do

This book isn't just about clearing out cupboards. It's about creating a new relationship with your space—and with yourself. It's about putting your home and your mind back on the same team.

In the chapters ahead, you'll find:

- A quiz to help you discover your **Clutter Personality** (Chapter 2)

- A step-by-step approach to clear every room in your home (Chapter 5)

- Tools for decluttering your **schedule, mind, and digital life** (Chapters 6 and 7)

- Strategies for letting go of **guilt and emotional attachment** (Chapter 8)

- A **21-day challenge** to reset your life with tiny, daily actions (Chapter 11)

And throughout it all, you'll be guided gently. No harsh rules. No judgment. Just encouragement, insight, and small, meaningful steps.

Your Reset Starts Now

You don't need to have it all figured out before you begin. You don't need to tidy everything in one weekend. All you need is a willingness to take one step.

In the next chapter, you'll take the Clutter Personality Quiz to discover what's really behind your clutter habits—and how to work with your natural tendencies, not against them.

Remember, this isn't just about getting rid of things. It's about making space—for peace, for clarity, and for the version of you that's been buried under too much.

Let's begin your reset.

Chapter 2: What Type of Clutterer Are You?

One of the most powerful things you can do before diving into any decluttering project is to **understand your relationship with clutter**. Not just what you own, but *why* you hold on to it. Because the truth is, clutter isn't just about habits—it's about emotion, identity, and mindset.

We all have different reasons for keeping things. Some of us are emotionally attached to objects that remind us of people, places or important moments. Others are driven by practicality or fear of waste. Some feel overwhelmed by time, energy, or decision-making, and so avoid decluttering altogether.

In this chapter, you'll take a **Clutter Personality Quiz** to identify your dominant style—and learn how to declutter in a way that works *with* your personality rather than against it.

There's no right or wrong type. No judgment here. Only insight and support.

Why This Matters

Knowing your clutter personality helps you:

- Anticipate emotional blocks before they trip you up
- Choose strategies that match your strengths
- Avoid guilt and shame when things feel hard
- Communicate better with others in your household
- Make sustainable changes instead of short-term fixes

Let's begin.

The Clutter Personality Quiz

Answer each question honestly. Choose the letter that best matches your usual response.

1. When I try to declutter, I often...

A. Get stuck because everything feels sentimental
B. Feel unsure—what if I need this later?
C. Put it off because I don't know where to start
D. Struggle to finish because I get distracted
E. Want to keep things for others or just in case someone else needs it

2. My home feels cluttered because...

A. I have emotional ties to many of my belongings
B. I like to keep things "just in case"
C. I'm too busy or overwhelmed to deal with it
D. I start projects but rarely finish them
E. I feel responsible for keeping things on behalf of others

3. Letting go of items makes me feel...

A. Sad—it's like losing a piece of the past
B. Nervous—I might regret it later
C. Exhausted—I don't even know where to begin
D. Frustrated—I lose focus and give up
E. Guilty—I might be throwing away something useful to someone

4. When I look at my clutter, I...

A. Feel emotional or nostalgic
B. Think, "But what if I need this?"
C. Feel tired just thinking about tackling it

D. Get distracted and jump to something else
E. Remember who gave it to me or who might want it

5. I tend to accumulate...

A. Sentimental items, cards, photos, schoolwork, mementos
B. Useful things like packaging, tools, supplies, and duplicates
C. Paperwork, laundry, everyday mess I don't have time to sort
D. DIY supplies, half-finished projects, impulse buys
E. Items other people didn't want but I couldn't throw away

6. My clutter makes me feel...

A. Emotionally overwhelmed—it's hard to face
B. Anxious about the future—I might need it
C. Tired and behind—like I'm never caught up
D. Frustrated—I start but can't finish
E. Burdened—like I'm carrying other people's stuff

7. My approach to sentimental items is...

A. I keep nearly everything—they're too special to lose
B. I try to keep some, but I worry about regretting it
C. I don't have time to go through them properly
D. I intend to sort them but get distracted or stuck
E. I keep them mostly for others, not for me

8. When I declutter, I usually...

A. Reminisce and get caught up in memories
B. Second-guess my choices and hang on "just in case"
C. Get overwhelmed and stop after a short time
D. Jump from area to area without a clear plan
E. Feel like I should ask permission to get rid of things

9. My biggest fear when decluttering is...

A. Losing something precious or irreplaceable
B. Needing something later and not having it
C. Starting something I can't finish
D. Realising how much time or money I've wasted
E. Offending someone by discarding something they gave me

10. I would describe my relationship with clutter as...

A. Deeply emotional—it's tied to who I am or who I love
B. Practical—I keep things because they might be useful
C. Chaotic—I'm too busy to manage it consistently
D. Messy—I have good intentions but lack follow-through
E. Complicated—I hold onto things for others, not always myself

Results: Tally your answers

Count how many times you answered A, B, C, D, or E.

- **Mostly A = The Sentimental Saver**
- **Mostly B = The Just-in-Case Keeper**
- **Mostly C = The Overwhelmed Avoider**
- **Mostly D = The Distracted Dabbler**
- **Mostly E = The Keeper for Others**

If you had a fairly even mix, you may have a **primary** and a **secondary** type, which is completely normal. Use the descriptions in the chapter to learn which strategies apply to you best.

Your Clutter Personality Types

A – The Sentimental Saver

You hold on to things that have emotional meaning. You see memories in objects and worry that letting go will feel like erasing part of your past.

- **Strengths**: Thoughtful, nostalgic, emotionally connected
- **Challenges**: Difficulty letting go of items tied to people or milestones
- **Helpful Strategies**:
  - Choose *representative items* (e.g. one drawing, not all of them)
  - Photograph items before parting with them
  - Create a memory box with limits (one per person or year)

You don't have to keep everything to honour your memories.

B – The Just-in-Case Keeper

You're practical and cautious. You keep things in case they're needed later, even if they haven't been used in years.

- **Strengths**: Resourceful, responsible, prepared
- **Challenges**: Struggles to let go due to fear of future regret
- **Helpful Strategies**:
  - Use a "quarantine box": store the item for 30–60 days. If you don't use it, it goes
  - Ask: *What's the worst that could happen if I didn't have this?*
  - Focus on what you use *regularly*, not what you might possibly use

Trust your present self more than your future fears.

C – The Overwhelmed Avoider

You feel swamped and unsure where to begin. Life is busy or stressful, and clutter feels like one more exhausting task.

- **Strengths**: Caring, committed, busy with meaningful things
- **Challenges**: Paralysis from overwhelm, lack of time or energy
- **Helpful Strategies**:
  - Use **short bursts**: 10–15 minutes is enough to start
  - Focus on *one drawer, not the whole room*
  - Start where you spend the most time (like your bedside table or kitchen counter)

Progress, not perfection, is your path forward.

D – The Distracted Dabbler

You start with energy, but don't finish. You jump between tasks or struggle to focus long enough to complete one area fully.

- **Strengths**: Energetic, creative, spontaneous
- **Challenges**: Difficulty sustaining attention and structure
- **Helpful Strategies**:
  - Use timers (Pomodoro method) to stay focused
  - Make decluttering a playlist-powered or podcast task
  - Declutter with a friend or accountability partner

Consistency beats intensity—small wins matter.

E – The Keeper for Others

You hold onto things out of guilt or obligation. You worry about waste, sentiment, or throwing away something that isn't "yours" to toss.

- **Strengths**: Generous, thoughtful, loyal
- **Challenges**: Feels guilt, inherits others' clutter, struggles with boundaries
- **Helpful Strategies**:
    - Ask yourself: *Do I actually want this in my home?*
    - Set clear boundaries with family about heirlooms or storage
    - Give yourself permission to let go of things that were never truly yours

You are not responsible for preserving everyone else's past.

Final Thoughts

Once you understand your clutter type, the process becomes far less intimidating. You're no longer trying to force yourself to fit someone else's method. Instead, you can work with your natural tendencies, your strengths, and your emotional wiring.

In the next chapter, we'll look at the mindset shifts that make all the difference—how to move beyond guilt, fear, and "what ifs," and start letting go with confidence and clarity.

But first, take a moment to pause and reflect on what you've learned about yourself.

Reset Ritual: Know Yourself to Reset Gently

Take five minutes to complete this ritual:

1. **Write down your dominant clutter type** and 2–3 things that resonate from the description.

2. **Note one small habit** that may be keeping you stuck (e.g. "I save every birthday card.")

3. **Finish this sentence:** *I want to reset because…*

4. **Take one deep breath**, and say to yourself:
    "I am not my clutter. I am allowed to let go."

Place this note somewhere visible—your fridge, mirror, or bedside. It's a reminder that this reset starts with understanding, not shame.

Chapter 3: Shift Your Mindset, Not Just Your Mess

Decluttering begins in the mind long before it shows up in the home. You can buy all the storage boxes and donation bags in the world, but if you're still holding on to guilt, fear, or perfectionism, you'll struggle to make meaningful progress. That's why a true reset doesn't start with cleaning—it starts with thinking differently.

If you've ever stood in front of a messy drawer and felt emotionally stuck, you're not alone. What's in our homes is often a mirror of what's going on inside. Our stuff can represent hopes, regrets, memories, or even unmet goals. So, when we declutter, we're not just tidying—we're confronting how we feel about the past, the future, and ourselves.

This chapter is about resetting the way you think about clutter—so that when you do start letting go, it feels freeing, not frightening.

Why Mindset Matters

So many people try to declutter by focusing on **what to get rid of**. They go in with a bin bag and a grim sense of duty. And yes, that can work—for a little while. But if your beliefs about your stuff don't change, the clutter comes back.

That's because our actions are driven by our thoughts. And if those thoughts are things like:

- "I might need this later."

- "It's a waste to throw it out."

- "It reminds me of when life was better."

- "What if I make the wrong decision?"

Then no matter how hard you try to clear the surface, something keeps pulling you back. Your clutter, in a way, becomes a comfort zone. It's familiar. Predictable. And letting go feels risky.

But here's the truth: **decluttering is not about deprivation. It's about liberation.**
It's not about becoming someone else—it's about coming back to yourself, unburdened.

Let's Shift the Story

Let's look at some of the most common thoughts that block decluttering—and reframe them with gentler, more helpful beliefs.

✗ *"I might need this one day."*

✓ **New thought:** *If I haven't needed it in the past year, I can trust that I'll be okay without it.*

This is the classic "just in case" fear. It's a form of future-proofing, but it comes at a cost: space, peace, and clarity today. Ask yourself: *Can I easily replace this if I ever do need it? Is the cost of keeping it higher than the risk of letting it go?*

✗ *"It's wasteful to throw it away."*

✓ **New thought:** *The waste has already happened. Keeping it doesn't change that.*

This one is powerful. Holding on to something you no longer use doesn't undo its cost or environmental impact. If it can still serve someone else, donating it gives it new life. If not, letting it go can still serve *you* by freeing up space and reducing your mental burden.

✗ *"It reminds me of a good time."*

✓ **New thought:** *The memory lives in me, not the object.*

Memories are precious. But not every item tied to a memory needs to be kept. Choosing one or two meaningful pieces—and letting go of the rest—allows you to honour the moment without being buried by it.

✗ *"I don't know where to start, so I won't."*

✅ **New thought:** *Small steps still count. I only need to do one thing today.*

Overwhelm is real, especially if you're juggling work, parenting, or just daily life. But a mindset of *all or nothing* leads to burnout or paralysis. The truth is, even ten minutes of progress is still progress. Your reset doesn't need to be fast—it needs to be consistent.

✗ *"I might regret it later."*

✅ **New thought:** *I trust myself to make good decisions now.*

Regret thrives on perfectionism—the idea that there's a "right" decision and anything else is failure. But letting go of something and later wishing you hadn't is not a disaster. It's just life. And most of the time, that regret never comes. What does come is relief.

Understanding Emotional Clutter

Physical clutter often has emotional roots. You might not be keeping something because it's useful—you're keeping it because it's **comforting**, or **familiar**, or tied to your identity.

Let's look at some common examples:

- **Clothes that don't fit** → Hope for who you once were or want to be

- **Gifts you don't love** → Guilt about rejecting someone's kindness

- **Craft supplies or tools** → Unused potential or hobbies you never had time for

- **Boxes of paperwork** → Fear of missing something important or letting go of control

These items carry emotional weight. They aren't just "things"—they represent parts of our inner world. And that's why decluttering them can feel so hard. But it can also be incredibly healing.

When you let go of a version of yourself you're no longer trying to be, you make space for the one you are becoming. When you release the guilt of unused gifts or failed projects, you gain clarity about what truly matters now.

♥ Permission to Let Go

Sometimes, the missing piece is simply **permission**. So if no one has said it to you before, let me say it now:

- You are allowed to let go of things, even if they were expensive.

- You are allowed to let go of gifts, even if someone meant well.

- You are allowed to let go of items tied to memories, while keeping the memory itself.

- You are allowed to need space.

- You are allowed to prioritise peace over perfection.

A Quick Reflection

Ask yourself:

- What story am I telling myself about why I need to keep this?

- Is this story still true—or is it an old belief I no longer need?

- What would I gain—not lose—by letting this go?

When you approach decluttering with curiosity instead of criticism, you create room for change.

Practical Mindset Tools

Here are some tools and questions you can use the next time you feel emotionally blocked:

The One-Year Rule:
Have I used this, worn this, or thought about this in the last year? If not, it's probably safe to let go.

The Replacement Rule:
If I let this go and needed it later, could I replace it easily and affordably? If yes, release it.

The Joy + Usefulness Rule:
Does this item bring me joy or serve a clear function? If not, its time may have passed.

The Memory Swap:
Can I take a photo of this item instead of keeping it? The memory stays, the clutter goes.

Reset Ritual: Your Let-Go List

This 5–10 minute ritual helps shift your mindset from fear to freedom.

1. **Find a quiet spot** and grab a piece of paper or notebook.

2. Title the page: *"Things I'm Ready to Release"*

3. List 5 items or types of items you've been holding onto—even if just mentally—that you're open to letting go of.

    o   They can be physical (like "old paperwork" or "clothes that don't fit")

    o   Or emotional (like "guilt about throwing out gifts")

4. Choose *one* item from the list to let go of this week.

5. Read this affirmation out loud or write it down:

"Letting go creates space for something better. I trust myself to know what I need now."

In the next chapter, we'll begin putting this mindset into action. You'll learn the **Reset Zone Method**—a simple, non-overwhelming way to start decluttering your space with clarity and confidence. No pressure, no perfection—just one zone at a time.

You're doing more than tidying. You're creating room to breathe.

Ready? Let's go.

Chapter 4: The Reset Zone Method

By now, you've explored how clutter affects your mind, identified your personal clutter personality, and started shifting the thoughts that hold you back. You might be feeling more ready than ever to take action—but still wondering, *Where on earth do I begin?*

The truth is, one of the biggest barriers to successful decluttering is trying to tackle too much at once. Standing in the middle of a messy room, unsure where to start, is a fast track to feeling overwhelmed. That's where the **Reset Zone Method** comes in.

This chapter introduces a simple, strategic way to declutter your home in manageable pieces—without the chaos, without the stress, and most importantly, **without the pressure to be perfect**.

What Is a Reset Zone?

A **Reset Zone** is a small, clearly defined space that you focus on fully before moving to the next.

Think:

- One drawer
- One shelf
- One corner of a room
- One countertop
- One digital folder

The idea is to **zoom in**, not zoom out. By choosing a micro-space instead of an entire room, you give yourself permission to start small—and win big.

Reset Zones work because they:

- Create instant, visible results
- Prevent decision fatigue

- Build confidence through momentum
- Turn decluttering into a habit, not a one-time event

You don't need to declutter your whole house in a weekend. You just need to reset one zone at a time.

How to Choose Your First Reset Zone

You might be tempted to start with the hardest or most cluttered area—but don't. Decluttering is like exercise: if you start too hard, you risk burning out. Start with a space that's **small and frequently used** so you can enjoy the benefits right away.

Here are some great first Reset Zones:

- Your bedside table
- A kitchen drawer
- Your bathroom shelf
- Your purse, bag or wallet
- The area around your kettle or coffee maker
- Your phone's home screen or app list

Pick a spot where success will make you smile.

The 5-Step Reset Zone Method

Once you've chosen your zone, follow these simple steps:

Step 1: Clear It Completely

Take everything out. Yes, everything. Lay it on a towel, table, or even the floor. Seeing the full contents helps you assess what's really there—how much you use, love, or even forgot existed.

Step 2: Wipe It Clean

Before anything goes back, give the space a physical reset. A quick wipe-down is symbolic as well as practical—it tells your brain, *this area is starting fresh.*

Step 3: Sort Into Three Simple Piles

Use this fast filter system:

- **Keep** (you use it, love it, or truly need it)
- **Let Go** (you don't use it, it's broken, expired, or unwanted)
- **Unsure** (you hesitate—place it in a decision box or revisit later)

Avoid overthinking. Trust your gut. Remember, you're not making forever decisions—you're simply deciding what belongs in *this space* today.

Step 4: Return With Intention

Only put back what truly fits the purpose of the space. Don't overload the area again. Let it breathe. Group similar items. Use containers or small dividers if helpful—but only *after* decluttering. Don't organise clutter. Reset it.

Step 5: Celebrate the Win

Yes, even if it's "just" one drawer. Step back. Breathe. Notice how it feels. That clear space is a signal to your brain: *progress is happening.*

The Magic of One Zone at a Time

One of the most satisfying things about the Reset Zone Method is that it builds **daily success into the process**. Each zone becomes a mini-win—a reminder that you *can* do this, and you *are* doing it.

Small resets ripple outward. Clear your bedside table, and suddenly your mornings feel calmer. Clear your kitchen counter, and cooking feels less chaotic. Reset your phone apps, and your brain feels less scattered.

The method also fits any lifestyle. Whether you have five minutes or 30, whether you live alone or share a space, whether you're tackling one zone a day or one a week—**it adapts to you.**

The Building Blocks of a Calm Home

As you begin resetting more zones, you'll start to notice something: your home begins to feel lighter. Less chaotic. More *yours*.

That's because Reset Zones become building blocks for a calmer life. Instead of frantically tidying when guests come over or feeling ashamed of cluttered corners, you're creating a home that feels purposeful and peaceful, bit by bit.

Your goal is not a "perfect" house—it's a space that supports how you *want to live*. And that begins with clearing what no longer serves you.

Common Questions & Reassurance

"What if I don't have time for even a drawer?"
You can do a mini reset. Try a 5-minute tidy of your bag, your phone, or your fridge door. Progress over perfection.

"What if I make the wrong decision?"
There are no perfect decisions, only useful ones. If you're unsure, create a *"decision box"*—store the item temporarily and revisit in 30 days.

"What if other people in my home undo my progress?"
Focus on **your** zones first—your bedside table, your desk, your phone. Your calm will influence others more than pressure ever could.

Start Small, Reset Often

Here are 10 Reset Zone ideas you can try over the next two weeks:

1. Your bathroom cabinet

2. A kitchen utensil drawer

3. Your desktop or downloads folder

4. Your wardrobe's top shelf

5. The area by your front door

6. Your handbag or wallet

7. The area around your TV or remote controls

8. A junk drawer (yes, the dreaded one!)

9. Your car glove box or centre console

10. Your inbox—start by deleting 50 emails or unsubscribing from 5 newsletters

Even doing **just one of these** can boost your mood and motivation.

Reset Ritual: Choose & Clear One Zone

This ritual takes just 10–20 minutes, but it delivers an instant mental lift.

1. **Choose your Reset Zone** – Keep it small and manageable (drawer, shelf, bag).

2. **Set a timer** for 15 minutes.

3. **Follow the 5 steps**: Empty, clean, sort, return, celebrate.

4. **Write down how it felt**: Use a journal or even your phone notes.

    o   What surprised you?

    o   What felt easy?

    o   What did it shift in your mood or space?

Finish with this affirmation:

"Progress is happening. One clear space at a time, I'm creating the life I want."

In the next chapter, we'll zoom out slightly and look at how to apply the Reset Zone Method **room by room**—with practical tips for bedrooms, kitchens, bathrooms, and more. This is where the reset starts to feel like *real change.*

Ready to go beyond drawers and into the heart of your home? Let's continue.

Chapter 5: Room-by-Room Reset

Once you've mastered the basics of the **Reset Zone Method**, you might feel ready to expand your reach. This chapter will help you do just that—without feeling overwhelmed or tempted to take on too much too fast.

Now we'll walk through how to apply this method to the most commonly cluttered areas of the home. Think of this as a **room-by-room map**, where each stop offers small, achievable wins that lead to big change.

You don't have to follow this in order. Start with whatever space is most important—or most frustrating—to you right now. What matters most is that you **start where the change will feel meaningful**.

The Bedroom: Your Calm Zone

Your bedroom should be the most restful space in your home. And yet for many people, it becomes a dumping ground: laundry, bags, unread books, and items that don't belong anywhere else.

Start with:

- Your bedside table

- The floor around your bed

- The top of your dresser

Quick Wins:

- Remove anything that doesn't support rest: paperwork, cluttered chargers, unfinished projects

- Keep only your essentials within arm's reach: lamp, book, water, one or two calming items

- Declutter under the bed—out of sight shouldn't mean out of mind

Why it matters:
A clear bedroom signals your body that it's safe to slow down. Even one decluttered nightstand can improve how you feel when you wake up.

The Wardrobe: A Fresh Start

Clothes can carry so many emotions—identity, weight changes, old roles, nostalgia. But your wardrobe should serve the *you of today*, not past or future versions of yourself.

Start with:

- One drawer
- One clothing rail
- Your shoes or accessories

Quick Wins:

- Try the *backwards hanger trick*: turn all hangers backward, and only flip them when you wear something. After 3 months, donate what hasn't been worn.
- Use the *one-in, one-out rule* moving forward
- Create a small "feel-good favourites" section you can always rely on

Why it matters:
A simplified wardrobe saves time, reduces decision fatigue, and helps you dress with more confidence and less stress.

The Kitchen: Function Over Fuss

The kitchen is a high-use zone, and clutter here can make daily life feel chaotic. This is where Reset Zones really shine—because even small clear-outs can transform your routine.

Start with:

- The cutlery drawer

- One food cupboard or spice rack

- The area around your kettle, toaster, or hob

Quick Wins:

- Clear expired food, duplicate gadgets, or stained Tupperware

- Create a daily-use drawer with go-to tools: scissors, spatula, peeler, etc.

- Keep countertops as clear as possible—visual space equals mental space

Why it matters:
When your kitchen flows easily, meals become smoother, mornings calmer, and the energy of your home more grounded.

The Bathroom: Simple and Soothing

Bathrooms collect clutter faster than we realise—half-used bottles, expired creams, old toothbrushes. But a quick bathroom reset can have a huge emotional payoff.

Start with:

- Your medicine cabinet or toiletry shelf

- The shower caddy or windowsill

- Under-sink storage

Quick Wins:

- Toss anything expired, unused, or sticky

- Group products by use: daily, weekly, occasional

- Limit open products—finish one before opening another

Why it matters:
This is where your day often starts and ends. A clean, calm bathroom makes routines feel intentional instead of rushed.

The Living Room: Space to Breathe

As a shared, high-traffic space, the living room can be tricky. It often becomes a catch-all for paperwork, toys, books, and forgotten items. Your goal here is to simplify and reclaim clarity—not aim for perfection.

Start with:

- The coffee table
- The TV stand or remote basket
- One shelf or storage unit

Quick Wins:

- Remove anything that belongs elsewhere
- Reduce decorative clutter—leave room for the eye to rest
- Limit "open storage" like baskets or trays that collect junk

Why it matters:
A calm living space invites relaxation, connection, and breathing room—both physically and emotionally.

The Home Office or Paper Zone

Even if you don't have a formal office, most homes have a place where paperwork collects: bills, receipts, notes from school, and lists. This area can quickly become a stress magnet.

Start with:

- Your desk drawer
- A "paper pile"

- Your planner or wall calendar

Quick Wins:

- Recycle anything expired or irrelevant
- Create one inbox tray for new papers
- Scan and digitise anything you don't need in hard copy

Why it matters:
When your paper clutter shrinks, your mental load does too.
Decision-making becomes easier, and you regain a sense of control.

The Digital Zones: Often Forgotten, Always Overwhelming

Your phone and laptop might not take up physical space—but they absolutely take up **mental space**. A quick digital declutter can boost your clarity, focus, and mood.

Start with:

- Your phone's home screen
- Email inbox
- Download or desktop folder

Quick Wins:

- Delete unused apps or move them into a folder
- Unsubscribe from five emails
- Archive everything older than 6 months (trust me, you won't miss it)
- Clear 10 photos or videos that you don't want or need

Why it matters:
Your digital life is a part of your mental environment. When it's clear, you think and feel better.

Reset Ritual: Choose a Room, Choose a Zone

1. Choose one room from this chapter that you feel drawn to reset.

2. Choose **one Reset Zone** within that room.

    o   Example: *Kitchen → Cutlery drawer*

    o   Example: *Bedroom → Bedside table*

3. Clear, clean, sort, return, and reflect.

4. Ask yourself:

    o   How does it feel to have this space reset?

    o   What other zone in this room could I try next?

    o   What time of day would I enjoy doing more of this?

Finish with this affirmation:

"One clear space at a time, I am creating a calm and supportive home."

In the next chapter, we'll explore how clutter doesn't just live in your home—it lives in your **mind**. You'll learn gentle ways to reset your internal world, let go of mental overload, and experience more focus and calm, without needing to meditate on a mountain.

Ready to go inward? Let's begin.

Chapter 6: Decluttering Your Mind

So far, we've focused on physical clutter—resetting drawers, rooms, and routines. But now it's time to look inward. Because the mess in our homes often mirrors the mess in our minds.

Mental clutter shows up in many forms. Worry, racing thoughts, overthinking, constant to-do lists, decision fatigue, and even guilt about what you haven't finished. You might be carrying old conversations, worries about the future, or simply a long list of everything you think you *should* be doing.

And just like physical clutter, mental clutter weighs you down. It makes it harder to focus, relax, or even enjoy the moment you're in.

Decluttering your mind doesn't mean achieving complete stillness or never thinking about anything stressful again. It means creating enough mental space to think clearly, feel grounded, and respond rather than react.

This chapter will help you gently reset your mental space using simple, sustainable techniques that work even if you're busy, distracted, or not naturally drawn to mindfulness.

What Does Mental Clutter Look Like?

Mental clutter is often invisible, but it affects your daily life in powerful ways. You may be carrying it if you notice any of the following:

- You wake up already feeling behind

- Your thoughts are constantly jumping from one thing to another

- You replay conversations or regrets on repeat

- You find it hard to make decisions, even small ones

- You struggle to be fully present, even in moments of rest

You might also feel mentally cluttered when you're trying to remember too many things at once. Our brains are not designed to be filing cabinets. Holding onto every task, deadline, or concern in your head creates tension, forgetfulness, and fatigue.

Just like your physical environment needs order, your mind needs room to breathe.

Why Mental Clutter Matters

When your mind is crowded, your nervous system is more easily triggered. You might find yourself feeling anxious, irritable, or emotionally drained. And because it's not always obvious what's causing the pressure, it can be hard to know how to fix it.

Decluttering your mind helps you:

- Improve focus and productivity
- Feel more emotionally regulated
- Sleep better
- Reduce stress and anxiety
- Increase your ability to enjoy the present moment
- Create clarity around what really matters

Mental space is just as important as physical space—and the two are deeply connected. That's why many people report feeling mentally lighter after tidying up a single drawer or corner. It's not just about the space. It's about what the space *represents*.

How to Declutter Your Mind

There's no one-size-fits-all method for creating mental clarity. Below are several simple tools you can try. Choose what fits best for you and your life.

1. The Brain Dump

This is one of the most powerful tools for clearing mental clutter. It's exactly what it sounds like: a chance to offload every thought, task, idea, or worry onto paper.

Grab a notebook and write down everything that's floating around in your head. Don't censor. Don't organise. Just empty it out.

What this does:

- Helps you stop holding everything in your memory
- Allows you to see your thoughts more objectively
- Creates space to prioritise or release what no longer matters

Try doing a brain dump in the evening to sleep better or on a Sunday evening to start the week feeling lighter.

2. Write a "Let Go" List

This is different from a to-do list. It's a list of things you're choosing not to carry anymore.

It might include:

- A regret or past decision
- A conversation that's been replaying in your mind
- A task that's been sitting on your list for months, but no longer matters
- Guilt about not being productive enough

Write them down, then cross them out one by one. Imagine yourself mentally releasing them as you go. This small act has a big emotional impact.

3. Limit Your Input

In the digital age, a major source of mental clutter is constant input—news, social media, notifications, messages, and entertainment. Our minds are rarely given space to be still or silent.

You don't have to cut everything out. But you can begin by setting boundaries:

- Turn off unnecessary phone notifications
- Avoid checking your phone first thing in the morning
- Have a "scroll-free" hour each evening
- Create a calming, input-free morning routine

The more you limit external noise, the more you can hear your own thoughts.

4. Create a Single Point of Focus

When your mind is overwhelmed, multitasking only makes it worse. Instead, choose one focus point at a time.

This could be:

- A single task at work
- A 10-minute walk with no distractions
- Washing the dishes slowly, mindfully
- Sitting down with a cup of tea and doing nothing else

Each time you bring your attention back to a single point, you're resetting your brain's focus muscle. Over time, it becomes easier to concentrate and easier to feel calm.

5. Simplify Your To-Do List

A long, scattered to-do list adds pressure to your day. Try this method instead:

- Write down *everything* you think you need to do.
- Then choose just *three* key tasks for the day.
- Highlight or star them. These are your priorities.
- If you complete them, you can choose more—but you don't have to.

This reduces overwhelm and creates a greater sense of achievement. Mental clutter often thrives when you feel like you're never "done." A simple, focused list helps you see your progress.

6. Create Thought Boundaries

Just as you would limit physical clutter in your home, you can limit how often you dwell on certain thoughts.

For example:

- Set a timer to worry. Give yourself 10 minutes to write out or reflect on your concerns. When the time's up, move on.

- Schedule a weekly "life admin" session to review your calendar, bills, or responsibilities, rather than thinking about them constantly.

Boundaries protect your mental space. They help you stop overthinking and start living more fully in the present.

Decluttering Your Mind Is an Ongoing Practice

This isn't about becoming a serene, thought-free person overnight. Your mind will still race. Life will still be busy. But each time you pause, breathe, and make space, you're practising a new habit—a habit of clarity, not chaos.

Mental clutter will creep back in just like physical clutter. But now, you'll have the tools to recognise it and reset.

As your mind becomes clearer, you'll likely notice:

- Your space feels more manageable

- You sleep better

- You enjoy moments without rushing through them

- You feel more like yourself again

It's not about doing more. It's about carrying less.

Reset Ritual: Clear Your Mind in 10 Minutes

Try this simple ritual whenever your mind feels overloaded. It works well at the end of the day or any time you want to reset.

1. Set a timer for 10 minutes.

2. Take out a notebook or piece of paper.

3. Do a full brain dump—everything on your mind. Write without stopping or editing.

4. Take a different coloured pen and highlight:

   o   What you can act on today

   o   What can wait

   o   What needs to be let go

5. Draw a line underneath your list. Write: *"I've cleared space. I trust myself to move forward with calm and clarity."*

Place your paper in a drawer or journal and leave it there. You've created space.

In the next chapter, we'll explore a clutter category many people overlook—your time. Because just like your home and your mind, your schedule can be reset too. When you declutter your calendar, you make space for rest, joy, and a life that feels more aligned with what you actually want.

Let's reset your time.

Chapter 7: Decluttering Your Schedule

Creating Time and Space to Breathe

When we think about clutter, we usually picture messy rooms or overstuffed cupboards. But there's another kind of clutter that weighs heavily on our well-being—**calendar clutter**. It's the back-to-back commitments, the endless to-do lists, and the mental juggling act of trying to keep up with everything.

If your days feel rushed, your weekends never feel restful, and you rarely have time to pause, your schedule might be just as cluttered as your kitchen drawer.

Decluttering your time is just as powerful as decluttering your home. In fact, it may be even more important. Because time isn't something we can buy more of. Once it's spent, it's gone. Creating a clearer, calmer schedule allows you to live more fully in the present, make room for what matters most, and reduce the constant feeling of being "on."

This chapter will guide you through the process of gently resetting your calendar and commitments, so your time begins to reflect your values—not just your obligations.

How Time Clutter Builds Up

Time clutter doesn't usually appear all at once. It builds slowly and silently. You agree to something small—a favour, a recurring meeting, a one-off event—and before you know it, your calendar is packed.

You might notice signs of time clutter if:

- You often say yes out of guilt or habit

- You struggle to find even 15 minutes to yourself

- You regularly cancel or reschedule things because you're overstretched

- You feel like you're busy all the time but rarely get anything meaningful done

- Your weekends leave you more tired than your weekdays

Many of us were taught to equate busyness with worth or productivity. But constant activity isn't the same as intentional living. In fact, too much busyness can drown out joy, creativity, and peace.

Decluttering your schedule isn't about doing nothing. It's about **doing less of what drains you and more of what lifts you**.

The Cost of a Cluttered Calendar

When your schedule is overstuffed, it affects more than just your time. It impacts:

Your energy: You feel depleted before the day is halfway through.

Your relationships: You're less present with loved ones, distracted or short-tempered.

Your health: Constant rushing can lead to sleep problems, anxiety, or burnout.

Your space: When time is tight, clutter tends to grow—laundry piles up, meals are rushed, and routines fall apart.

Just like physical clutter fills your home with noise and friction, schedule clutter fills your days with stress and urgency. It leaves no room to breathe.

How to Begin Decluttering Your Time

Let's walk through a practical way to reset your schedule using the same principles you've applied to physical decluttering.

Step 1: Look at the Whole Picture

Grab your planner, calendar app, or a blank piece of paper. Write down all your regular time commitments for the week.

Include:

- Work hours or projects

- School runs or children's activities

- Household tasks and errands

- Appointments, meetings, or social events

- Volunteering, favours, or unpaid roles

- Digital time—how much goes to scrolling, streaming, or messaging?

Once it's on paper, you can see where your time is really going.

Step 2: Sort Your Commitments

Now use a simple filter:

- **Keep** – Things that energise you, reflect your values, or are essential

- **Let Go** – Things you do out of guilt, habit, or obligation, but no longer serve you

- **Re-evaluate** – Things that might be adjusted, delegated, or postponed

Look at each activity and ask:
Does this add value to my life, or just add pressure?

It's okay to let go of good things to make space for better things.

Step 3: Create Time Boundaries

Once you've identified what needs to change, put up some gentle but firm boundaries.

Try:

- Blocking off one evening a week for rest or family

- Saying no to one new commitment this month

- Taking one meeting off your calendar that isn't essential

- Giving yourself 10-minute transition gaps between tasks

Protecting your time is an act of self-respect. When you create boundaries, you teach others (and yourself) that your time has value.

Step 4: Build in White Space

Just like a well-designed room needs empty space, so does your schedule.

Give yourself unstructured time each day—even if it's only 20 minutes. You don't need to *do* anything with it. That's the point.

White space gives you time to:

- Think clearly
- Be creative
- Pause and enjoy your surroundings
- Rest your nervous system
- Catch up gently if the day runs over

If your whole day is packed to the edge, even a small bump can throw everything off. White space creates flexibility.

Permission to Slow Down

Slowing down isn't lazy. It's a conscious choice to live at a pace that feels good, not just productive. The world will always demand more of your time than you can give. So your job is to decide what truly deserves it.

You are allowed to:

- Say no to invitations, even if you feel guilty
- Cancel something if your body or mind needs rest
- Prioritise quiet evenings over social events
- Stop rushing through your life

Your value doesn't come from how much you get done. It comes from how intentionally you live.

Let Go of the "Busy Badge"

Somewhere along the line, many of us learned that being constantly busy meant we were important, useful, successful. But busy isn't a badge of honour. It's a warning sign.

If your schedule is full but your heart feels empty, it's time for a reset.

Letting go of busyness opens the door to deeper presence, more joy, and a life that's spacious enough to breathe.

Time Resets to Try This Week

Here are a few simple ways to declutter your schedule right now:

- Cancel or reschedule one unnecessary appointment
- Decline one invitation that doesn't align with your needs
- Set aside one "protected" hour for yourself this week
- Batch errands or tasks to reduce running around
- Spend one evening without screens or commitments
- Take a full lunch break—even 20 minutes without multitasking

Small shifts like these create a ripple effect. As you feel the benefits of space, you'll naturally begin to protect it more fiercely.

Reset Ritual: Clear Your Calendar Gently

Try this simple 10-minute reset to release calendar clutter and reclaim your time.

1. Take out your planner, app, or notebook.
2. List every commitment or regular activity you have over the next seven days.
3. Next to each one, write a symbol or short note:

   o Keep

   o Let Go

- Re-evaluate

4. Choose one activity to remove, cancel, or postpone.

5. Choose one time block to protect for rest, fun, or reflection.

6. Write this at the top of your week:
   "I am allowed to rest. I am allowed to protect my time."

Even one small change can create powerful relief.

In the next chapter, we'll explore what it means to let go of the deeper emotional attachments behind clutter. You'll learn how to release with kindness, honour your memories, and move forward feeling lighter and more free.

Let's begin the emotional side of the reset.

Chapter 8: Letting Go of Emotional Attachments

Clearing Space Without Losing What Matters

Some things are easy to declutter—expired food, broken pens, old receipts. You toss them and move on. But then there are the things that stop you in your tracks. A baby blanket, a wedding invitation, a school report with a star at the top. Things that hold a story, a memory, a feeling.

This is the emotional layer of clutter—the part that doesn't respond to logic or storage solutions. You may know you don't *need* the item, but something in you resists letting it go. It feels like throwing away part of your identity or erasing a special moment.

In this chapter, we'll gently explore how to let go of emotionally charged items with care, not force. You'll learn how to honour the past without living in it, and how to create space without losing what truly matters.

Because decluttering is not just a practical act—it's an emotional one too.

Why Emotional Items Are So Hard to Release

Emotional clutter connects us to:

- Who we were
- Who we love
- Where we've been
- Who we hoped to become

Letting go of a physical object can feel like letting go of a memory, a role, or even a relationship. It can bring up grief, nostalgia, regret, or guilt.

Some common examples include:

- Childhood artwork or schoolbooks

- Clothes from a past phase of life

- Gifts from people you're no longer close to

- Souvenirs from travels or special events

- Letters, cards, or diaries

Often, we keep these things not because they bring us joy now, but because they *once did*. Or because we feel we should. But when these items take up too much space, physically or emotionally, they begin to weigh us down instead of lifting us up.

My Experience as a Sentimental Saver

As someone who identifies as a sentimental saver, I've been there. When I moved house with my daughter, I found boxes filled with everything from her early school paintings to tiny clay animals with missing limbs. I had saved every note, drawing, and handmade card—telling myself that one day we'd look through them together.

But the truth was, there were too many to ever fully enjoy. The special pieces were buried beneath piles of everything. I realised I wasn't preserving memories—I was burying them in clutter.

Letting go wasn't easy. But I found that when I chose carefully— keeping a few treasured items and releasing the rest—I could honour her childhood *and* give us both a home with space to grow.

How to Let Go Without Guilt

If you struggle to release emotional items, you're not alone. The following strategies can help you let go gently, with grace.

1. Keep Representative Pieces

You don't need to keep every item to honour a memory. Choose one or two meaningful items that best represent a time, person, or feeling. Let those stand in for the rest.

For example:

- One outfit from your child's baby clothes

- A single letter that captures a relationship

- A few standout pieces of artwork instead of dozens

Less truly can be more. It allows you to appreciate what you keep rather than store it out of guilt.

2. Take Photos Before You Let Go

Sometimes the physical object isn't necessary to keep—the memory is enough. Taking a photo allows you to preserve the story without keeping the space.

You can even create a digital memory folder or photo book of the items you release. This is especially helpful for bulky items like crafts, toys, or souvenirs.

3. Create a Memory Box—with Limits

Choose a small, beautiful box or container for sentimental items. Give yourself clear boundaries: one box per person, or one box per chapter of life.

When the box is full, it's time to review and edit. This helps ensure you're keeping only what truly matters to your heart, not your habit.

4. Ask Gentle Questions

When you're unsure about letting something go, ask:

- What does this item represent to me?
- Do I love the item itself—or the memory it's tied to?
- Does keeping this help me move forward—or keep me stuck in the past?

There are no wrong answers—only deeper awareness.

5. Give Items a Second Life

Some items feel too valuable to simply throw away—but you still don't want to keep them. Consider donating, gifting, or repurposing them.

Ideas:

- Turn artwork into a calendar or collage

- Give a loved item to someone who will use and enjoy it

- Donate memorabilia to a local charity shop or school

Letting go is easier when you know something will be appreciated elsewhere.

Grieving While Decluttering

Sometimes, decluttering stirs up grief—not just for people or moments we've lost, but for the versions of ourselves we've outgrown.

You might grieve:

- A relationship that's ended

- A role you no longer hold (like parent of a young child)

- A dream that didn't happen

- A body or phase of life that has changed

This is normal. Letting go is not just about stuff—it's about identity. It's okay to pause, to cry, to feel. It's okay to say goodbye to a season of life.

Letting go doesn't mean forgetting. It means making space for what comes next.

When It's Just Not Time Yet

There may be things you're not ready to release—and that's okay too. You don't have to declutter everything at once. You don't have to force closure.

If something feels too raw or sacred, set it aside in a "revisit later" box. Schedule a date to come back to it in a few months, or when life feels more spacious. This gives you permission to pause, without abandoning your progress.

Honouring Without Holding

You can honour the past without holding on to every part of it. You can cherish people and memories without storing physical reminders in every cupboard and drawer.

Think of it this way: space is also sacred. The room you create in your home and mind is what allows *new memories* to be made.

You are not dishonouring your past by letting go. You are making space for your future.

Reset Ritual: A Gentle Release

Set aside 15 minutes for this quiet ritual. Choose a calm moment when you can be undisturbed.

1. Choose one sentimental item you've been holding on to.

2. Hold it in your hands. Reflect on what it means to you.

3. If you're ready, take a photo or write a few words about the memory it represents.

4. Say thank you to the item—for what it gave you, reminded you of, or helped you through.

5. Let it go. Donate, recycle, or release it with care.

6. Pause and breathe. Notice how you feel.

Write this sentence in a journal or on a slip of paper:
"I carry the memory, not the item. I am allowed to keep the love and release the weight."

In the next chapter, we'll shift focus to sustainability—how to stop clutter from coming back. Because once you've done all this work to clear space, you'll want it to stay that way. Let's build systems that stick.

Chapter 9: Systems That Keep You Clear

Simple Habits for a Clutter-Free Life

You've done the work. You've cleared drawers, tackled emotional items, and created space in your calendar and your mind. Now comes the part most people forget—or skip altogether.

Maintenance.

Because even the clearest space can quietly refill with clutter if you don't have systems to support your progress. Think of it like brushing your teeth: doing it once won't keep them clean forever. But with simple, regular habits, things stay fresh with much less effort.

In this chapter, we'll explore practical systems and routines that help keep clutter from creeping back in. These aren't complicated or time-consuming. In fact, they're the opposite. They're designed to save you time, reduce decision fatigue, and keep your home and mind feeling clear—long after your big reset is complete.

Why Clutter Creeps Back

Decluttering is often seen as a one-off task—something you do once every few years when things get overwhelming. But in reality, clutter tends to return for a few common reasons:

- You haven't adjusted the habits that caused it
- There's no "home" for new items
- You're still saying yes to too much
- You're not regularly reviewing or resetting
- Life simply gets busy, and mess builds up silently

That's why a few small, consistent actions can make a huge difference. They stop clutter before it starts and help your space support your life—not compete with it.

The Power of Systems Over Willpower

If you've ever tried to stay tidy through sheer determination, you've probably discovered that willpower runs out. Life happens. Routines slip. You get tired. That's normal.

What you need is not more effort, but **better systems**.

A system is simply a habit or process that works for you, even when you're not feeling particularly motivated. It's something that happens automatically, like hanging your keys in the same place every day or resetting your desk before you finish work.

Good systems don't require constant thinking. They remove the need for decision-making by creating default behaviours. Over time, these become second nature—and your home stays clearer with far less effort.

Let's look at a few systems that can help.

1. The One-Minute Reset Rule

If something takes less than one minute to put away, do it immediately.

Hang up your coat. Rinse the dish. Put the charger back in the drawer. These tiny actions prevent the "I'll do it later" pile from ever forming.

You don't need to organise everything all the time—just handle the small tasks in the moment. It makes a surprising difference.

2. Create a Home for Everything

One of the fastest ways clutter builds up is when items don't have a clear place to live. Instead, they float around on surfaces or end up in catch-all drawers.

The solution? Assign everything a home.

That means:

- A specific basket for mail
- A shelf for books-in-progress
- A drawer for tech chargers

- A tray for keys and sunglasses

Once something has a home, it becomes easier to return it there without thinking.

If you can't find a home for something, it's a sign it may not belong in your space.

3. The Evening Reset

Take 10 minutes in the evening to reset the main living areas of your home.

Tidy the sofa cushions. Clear the kitchen surfaces. Put away anything that wandered during the day.

This short ritual helps you start the next day with a clean slate. It signals closure, calm, and control. You don't have to tidy the whole house—just give your environment a gentle refresh.

Even better, involve your family or housemates. A team reset makes the work lighter and reinforces shared responsibility.

4. Weekly Review and Release

Pick one day a week—maybe Sunday afternoon or Monday morning—to review and release anything unnecessary.

Scan your fridge, bag, inbox, and schedule. Ask:

- What's expired or no longer useful?

- What can be let go, cancelled, or rescheduled?

- What didn't work last week—and how can I reset it?

Think of this as a regular tidy-up for your whole life—not just your kitchen. It keeps you feeling on top of things and prevents overwhelm from creeping back in.

5. Practice the "One In, One Out" Rule

This simple rule can prevent future clutter without needing constant purging.

Whenever something new comes into your home—clothing, gadgets, books—let something else go. This keeps your space in balance and encourages more mindful purchasing.

You might also extend this to digital clutter. Download a new app? Delete one you no longer use. Subscribe to a newsletter? Unsubscribe from one you never open.

This mindset helps maintain space and clarity without relying on big clean-ups.

6. Set Boundaries for Stuff

Have clear limits for the categories of items most likely to multiply.

For example:

- One box of sentimental items

- One shelf for beauty products

- One drawer for tech accessories

- One small basket for toys in the living room

When that space fills, it's time to review and reset. Limits aren't about restriction—they're about clarity and control.

7. Seasonal Resets

Each season brings a natural opportunity to check in with your space and your life.

At the start of a new season, take a few hours to review:

- Wardrobes

- Outdoor gear

- Paperwork and admin

- Calendars and commitments

What worked last season might not serve you in the next. By reviewing and adjusting quarterly, you stay flexible, intentional, and clear.

Progress, Not Perfection

The goal of these systems isn't to create a perfect home. It's to support a life that feels lighter, calmer, and more aligned with who you are now.

There will still be weeks when life gets messy. That's okay. These systems are here to help you bounce back more easily—not feel bad when things aren't pristine.

A clutter-free life is not a spotless one. It's a life where your things support you, not stress you. Where your space reflects your values and leaves room for rest, creativity, and joy.

Reset Ritual: Your Weekly Reset Plan

Take 15 minutes this week to create your personalised reset system.

1. Choose one or two of the systems above to try for the next seven days.

2. Write them down and put them somewhere visible—a sticky note, your planner, or the fridge.

3. Commit to a daily "mini-reset" at a time that suits your routine (morning, lunch break, before bed).

4. Reflect at the end of the week:

   o What worked well?

   o What felt too much?

   o What would I like to adjust?

Finish by writing this sentence in your notebook or journal:
"I am building habits that support the life I want. I don't need to be perfect—I just need to keep going."

In the next chapter, we'll look at what happens when you share a space with others who may not be on the same decluttering journey. Because while you can reset your own habits, shared spaces bring unique challenges—and beautiful opportunities to lead by example.

Let's talk about decluttering when others aren't on board.

Chapter 10: When Others Aren't On Board

Decluttering Shared Spaces Without Conflict

Decluttering is often portrayed as a solo journey—but for many of us, that's far from reality. You might live with a partner, children, parents, flatmates, or all of the above. And while you may feel ready to clear the clutter and embrace a simpler way of living, not everyone in your home may feel the same.

Maybe your partner can't part with anything "just in case." Maybe your teenager leaves everything on the floor. Maybe your parent holds on to decades of items "because they might be valuable one day."

It's one thing to reset your own belongings. It's another to navigate the emotional and practical dynamics of shared spaces, different values, and clashing expectations.

But it's absolutely possible.

This chapter will help you find peace—not just in your home, but in your relationships. You'll learn how to lead by example, set clear boundaries, and encourage gentle cooperation rather than tension or control.

Because a clutter-free life isn't just about stuff—it's about how we live together with kindness and respect.

Why Others May Resist Decluttering

Before you start conversations or actions, it helps to understand why someone might resist decluttering in the first place. Resistance doesn't always come from laziness or stubbornness. It often stems from emotion, habit, or fear.

Some common reasons people hold on to things:

- **Sentimentality** – Emotional attachment to memories and identity

- **Fear of regret** – Worry about needing something later

- **Scarcity mindset** – Belief that resources should never be wasted

- **Overwhelm** – Feeling they don't have time, energy, or skill to sort things out

- **Control** – Clutter as a way of feeling safe or in charge

Recognising these deeper roots helps you approach the issue with more empathy and less frustration. When someone resists change, it's often because they feel unsafe, not because they're trying to block you.

What You Can (and Can't) Control

It's tempting to want to "fix" everyone's clutter. To clear out their wardrobes, tidy their papers, or clean their shelves when they're not looking. But this usually backfires.

Even if your intentions are good, decluttering someone else's belongings without consent can damage trust. It often leads to resentment, and in some cases, real emotional harm—especially if the items held deep meaning.

Here's what you *can* control:

- Your own belongings

- Your attitude and habits

- Your personal zones within the shared home

- The tone of your conversations

And here's what you *can't* control:

- Other people's readiness to let go

- Their emotional responses to clutter

- Their willingness to change

Let go of the need to convince, and instead focus on *influence*— through example, communication, and compassion.

Start with What's Yours

The most effective way to influence others is to start with yourself.

Clear your own clutter first:

- Your clothes
- Your desk
- Your side of the wardrobe
- Your digital life
- Any areas you can manage without asking permission

Let your own progress speak louder than words. When people see how much lighter and calmer you feel, they may become curious. That's when they're more open to trying it for themselves.

This is especially helpful with children or reluctant partners. They may resist being told what to do, but they'll often model what they see.

Define and Respect Personal Zones

One of the simplest and most respectful ways to reduce tension around clutter is to define clear zones in your home.

Identify:

- **Shared spaces** (e.g. kitchen, living room, bathroom)
- **Personal spaces** (e.g. bedroom areas, desks, shelves)
- **Neutral or "wild" zones** where flexibility is needed (e.g. kids' play areas)

For shared spaces, agree on a minimum baseline. For example:

- Dishes cleaned daily
- Surfaces wiped clear each evening
- No piles on the kitchen table

For personal spaces, allow autonomy. Your partner may keep a messy desk. Your teenager's room may not look like a magazine spread. If it's their zone, let it be theirs—unless it affects your safety or well-being.

This balance creates mutual respect and reduces the temptation to micromanage.

Talk, Don't Lecture

If you want to invite someone into the decluttering process, approach it gently. Avoid blame or ultimatums. Instead, focus on how clutter makes *you* feel, and ask for their perspective too.

Try phrases like:

- "I've been working on simplifying my space—it's made me feel so much clearer. Would you be open to talking about doing something similar together?"

- "I know we have different styles. Can we find a way to make the living room feel calmer for both of us?"

- "Would it be okay if I helped you go through this one shelf, just to see what's in it?"

Ask. Don't assume. Invite. Don't demand. When people feel heard, they're far more likely to participate.

Offer Gentle Support

If someone expresses willingness to declutter but doesn't know how to start, offer to sit with them or help guide the process.

You might:

- Set a timer for 15 minutes and tackle one drawer

- Help them make a "keep," "let go," and "maybe" pile

- Offer a reward or break afterward

- Celebrate small wins together

Be patient. Decluttering can feel vulnerable. Your role is not to rush them—it's to be present and supportive.

Focus on Shared Values, Not Standards

Sometimes, arguments around clutter stem from differences in values. One person wants the home to look neat and streamlined. Another values comfort, creativity, or having everything in sight.

Instead of pushing for uniformity, focus on shared values:

- Do you both want the space to feel welcoming?

- Do you both want to spend less time cleaning?

- Do you both value saving money, time, or energy?

Let these values guide your conversations and decisions. It's not about being right. It's about building a home that works for everyone in it.

Let Go of the Fantasy Family

One final challenge: many of us cling to clutter because we hold onto a vision of the "ideal" household—the one where everyone is organised, helpful, motivated, and always in sync.

But real families and households are messy. People are different. Life happens.

Let go of the fantasy version of your home and embrace the real one. It doesn't need to be perfect to be peaceful.

Instead of fighting what you can't change, focus on what you *can* influence—your space, your mood, your energy.

Sometimes, simply making peace with what is brings more clarity than trying to fix everything.

Reset Ritual: A Conversation for Connection

This week, choose one person you share space with and open a gentle conversation about your shared home.

1. Begin by sharing your own journey:

   o Why you've been decluttering

   o How it's made you feel

   o What you're hoping for moving forward

2. Ask for their thoughts:

   o How do they feel about the home right now?

   o Is there anything they'd like to change—or keep the same?

   o Are there any areas they'd like help with?

3. Choose one shared zone (e.g. hallway, kitchen shelf) to review together.

4. Agree on a few small changes that support both of you.

5. End the conversation with appreciation:

   o "Thank you for listening. I really value sharing this space with you."

Write down this affirmation:
"We can create a peaceful home through shared respect and small steps."

In the next chapter, we'll take a look at what happens after the reset—how to live in your new space with freedom, ease, and intention. Because this isn't just about letting go. It's about learning how to truly live with less, for good.

Chapter 11: Life After the Reset

Living with Less, and Loving It

You've let go of clutter. You've created calm corners, simplified your schedule, and made more space in your home—and in your head. You've worked hard to reset not only your environment, but also your mindset, your habits, and even your relationships.

Now what?

This chapter is about what happens after the big changes. The shift from *decluttering* to *living decluttered*. It's one thing to clear a space. It's another to embrace the stillness, ease, and freedom that follows—and trust that you don't need to fill it back up again.

If decluttering was about release, this next phase is about *enjoyment*. It's about fully living in the simpler, more spacious life you've created—and allowing that clarity to guide how you move forward.

Because a reset isn't just a one-time act. It's a foundation for a new way of being.

Noticing the Shift

Once the bulk of your decluttering is complete, there's often a moment when you realise: *I feel different*. The noise has quietened. The house feels more breathable. You're not digging through piles to find what you need. You're not constantly catching up or cleaning up.

Instead, you're:

- Waking up feeling lighter

- Moving through your home with more ease

- Spending less time maintaining and more time enjoying

- Feeling proud of your space instead of overwhelmed by it

- Making more intentional choices about what enters your life

It's subtle at first—but the shift is powerful.

For many people, this change doesn't just affect their home. It spills over into their work, their relationships, and their wellbeing. Because once you're no longer distracted by the mess, you can begin to focus on what matters most.

Trusting That Less Is Enough

Living with less can feel strange at first. There may be moments when the clear spaces feel too empty or too quiet. You might even feel the urge to refill them—buy new things, take on more tasks, or return to familiar habits.

This is completely normal. Our culture often encourages us to keep accumulating—whether it's stuff, productivity, or experiences. We're taught that more is better.

But when you've been through a reset, you begin to see the beauty in **enough.** You realise that peace doesn't come from filling every corner. It comes from choosing what *really* belongs there.

So when you feel the itch to add more, pause. Ask yourself:

- What feeling am I chasing?

- Will this truly add value—or is it a reflex?

- Am I responding to a need or a habit?

You are allowed to enjoy your home as it is. You are allowed to sit with space, silence, and simplicity—and know it's more than enough.

Living Intentionally

One of the great gifts of decluttering is the mental space it creates for intentional living. When you're no longer consumed by what to clean, buy, or manage, you can begin to ask deeper questions.

- What kind of life do I want to live in this space?

- What rhythms feel supportive and sustainable?

- How do I want to spend my time, energy, and attention?

- Who do I want to share this space with—and how do I want them to feel here?

Living intentionally means making choices that align with your values. It doesn't mean you have to have it all figured out. It simply means you act with awareness, not autopilot.

Now that your home is clearer, you have the space to notice what you want to welcome in—not just what you want to keep out.

Space Is a Gift

When you create space in your home, you make room for so much more than physical things.

You make space for:

- Creativity

- Rest

- Connection

- Spontaneity

- Growth

You stop managing clutter and start engaging with life.

Your kitchen becomes a place to cook slowly.
Your bedroom becomes a place to genuinely rest.
Your living room becomes a space to gather, laugh, and be present.
Your calendar reflects what matters, not just what's urgent.

Decluttering doesn't strip your life down. It lifts it up.

Staying Clear Without Perfection

A reset doesn't mean your home will never get messy again. Life is dynamic. Kids leave shoes out. Paper builds up. Unexpected events throw routines off.

That's not failure. That's life.

What matters is that you now know how to *reset*. You know how to come back to centre, quickly and gently. You've built habits that support clarity, and you know that a single shelf reset can bring back calm when things feel chaotic.

Instead of chasing perfection, focus on rhythm. Let your space evolve with your life. If clutter begins to build again, it's just a signal—it's time for another small reset.

And this time, you know exactly how to do it.

Gratitude for the Journey

As you step into this next phase, take a moment to acknowledge how far you've come.

You've made hard decisions.
You've let go of what no longer serves you.
You've honoured your memories while creating space for new ones.
You've learned how to protect your time, your energy, and your peace.

That's something to be deeply proud of.

Decluttering isn't just about changing your space. It's about changing your story. And now, you get to write a new one—one that feels lighter, freer, and more aligned with who you truly are.

Reset Ritual: Welcome In the New

Take 15 minutes to reflect and set an intention for your life after the reset.

1. Sit in a space you've recently decluttered. Notice how it feels.

2. Take a notebook or journal and answer the following prompts:

   o What have I let go of that no longer serves me?

   o What have I gained through this process—physically, emotionally, or mentally?

   o What do I want to invite into my life now that there's space for it?

3. Write a one-sentence intention:
   "In this next chapter, I will create space for _____."

4. Place this sentence somewhere visible—a note on your fridge, a sticky note by your mirror, or saved as a phone background.

Let this be your quiet commitment to yourself. A reminder that your reset wasn't just about removing things—it was about *making space for what matters most*.

In the next and final chapter, we'll bring everything together with a simple but powerful tool: the **21-Day Decluttering Reset Challenge**. This is your chance to build momentum, reinforce your habits, and experience lasting change—one day, one step at a time.

You've done the deep work. Now let's make it stick.

Chapter 12: The 21-Day Decluttering Reset Challenge

Make Simplicity a Lasting Part of Your Life

You've reset your space, rethought your routines, and reconnected with what truly matters. But as with all positive change, the real magic happens when you keep showing up—one small choice at a time.

This final chapter is your invitation to solidify everything you've learned. It's not about doing more. It's about doing a little—consistently.

Introducing the **21-Day Decluttering Reset Challenge**: a focused, flexible plan to help you stay on track, strengthen your habits, and keep your home and mind clear. Each day gives you one small task—nothing overwhelming, nothing time-consuming. Just a daily dose of clarity.

Why 21 days? Because science suggests it takes about three weeks to create a new habit. And by showing up each day in a simple way, you'll begin to feel that calm and clarity becoming part of your daily rhythm.

This challenge is designed to be encouraging, not exhausting. Skip a day? No problem. Start again when you're ready. The goal isn't perfection—it's momentum.

Let's begin.

How to Use This Challenge

- **One task per day** – Each task takes around 10–20 minutes.

- **Work at your own pace** – You can follow the days in order, skip ahead, or repeat days that feel useful.

- **Celebrate small wins** – Every item let go, every drawer reset, every mindful pause is progress.

- **Use your reset rituals** – Each day ends with a simple reflection or intention.

- **Repeat as needed** – You can return to this challenge whenever life feels cluttered again.

The 21-Day Decluttering Reset Challenge

Day 1: Declutter your bag or purse
Empty it completely, wipe it out, and only put back what you use daily.

Reset Ritual:
"I start with what I carry. I choose lightness."

Day 2: Clear your bedside table
Remove anything that doesn't support rest. Keep it calm and simple.

Reset Ritual:
"My sleep space is a sanctuary. I protect it with care."

Day 3: Do a five-minute brain dump
Write down everything on your mind—no filtering, no editing.

Reset Ritual:
"I release the mental clutter. I make space to think clearly."

Day 4: Tidy one kitchen drawer
Pick one drawer or shelf. Toss anything expired, broken, or unused.

Reset Ritual:
"One small space, one big breath of fresh energy."

Day 5: Sort your inbox or notifications
Unsubscribe from five emails or turn off unhelpful alerts.

Reset Ritual:
"My attention is precious. I direct it with purpose."

Day 6: Donate five items of clothing
Choose five things you no longer wear and send them on their way.

Reset Ritual:
"I dress for today—not for the past."

Day 7: Reclaim a cluttered surface
Choose one surface (coffee table, counter, desk) and clear it completely.

Reset Ritual:
"I choose clear space to breathe, think, and live."

Day 8: Create a memory box
Gather sentimental items into one defined container.

Reset Ritual:
"I honour my memories with care—not chaos."

Day 9: Declutter your schedule
Cancel or reschedule one task or commitment you no longer need.

Reset Ritual:
"My time reflects what matters most."

Day 10: Declutter your car (if you have one)
Remove rubbish, items that don't belong, or anything unused.

Reset Ritual:
"I move through life with clarity and calm."

Day 11: Organise your bathroom shelf
Check expiration dates and remove anything you haven't used in months.

Reset Ritual:
"I start and end my day with simplicity."

Day 12: Set a phone-free window
Choose one time today (e.g. first hour of the morning) to be phone-free.

Reset Ritual:
"Stillness is my strength. Presence is my power."

Day 13: Let go of one "maybe" item
Pick one item you've been undecided about—and make a decision.

Reset Ritual:
"I trust myself to release what no longer serves me."

Day 14: Reset your wardrobe
Choose 10 things you love and make them visible and accessible.

Reset Ritual:
"My clothes reflect who I am now—not who I was."

Day 15: Reset your digital space
Clear your desktop, phone home screen, or downloads folder.

Reset Ritual:
"My digital space supports my clarity and creativity."

Day 16: Revisit your reset goals
Read through your journal or notes from earlier in the book. What progress can you celebrate?

Reset Ritual:
"I honour how far I've come. I continue with ease and grace."

Day 17: Create a "donate" bag or box
Keep it somewhere visible for the week. Add to it daily.

Reset Ritual:
"I release gently, generously, and gratefully."

Day 18: Do a 10-minute evening tidy
Set a timer and do a calm reset of your main living space.

Reset Ritual:
"I end the day with intention and peace."

Day 19: Write a "not-to-do" list
Write down 5 things you will stop doing to protect your energy and time.

Reset Ritual:
"Simplifying is an act of self-respect."

Day 20: Share your progress
Tell a friend, partner, or journal entry what's changed for you.

Reset Ritual:
"I am proud of this journey. I share it with love."

Day 21: Reflect and reset again
Take 10 minutes to reflect. What's changed? What's next? What does "enough" now look like for you?

Reset Ritual:
"This is not the end. It's the beginning of a clearer, calmer way of life."

You Did It

You've reset not just your home—but your habits, your pace, your priorities. You've made space for ease, clarity, and connection. That's worth celebrating.

Decluttering isn't something you finish. It's something you learn to live with—gently, joyfully, and on your own terms. Now that you've made space, you get to decide what you invite in. Choose well. Choose slowly. Choose what supports the life you truly want.

And if life gets messy again—as it always does—you now know exactly how to begin again. With one drawer. One minute. One breath.

You are never behind. You are always allowed to reset.

Thank you for sharing this journey.

Afterword

You Already Know How to Begin Again

If you're reading this, you've come a long way.

You've opened drawers that had been avoided for years. You've asked hard questions about what really matters. You've cleared not only the clutter from your home but also the heaviness from your heart. You've learned to let go—with love, not guilt.

And now, you stand in a space that feels different. Lighter. Quieter. Yours.

But most importantly, you've discovered something powerful: **you don't need to be perfect to make real, lasting change**. You only need to keep coming back to what works.

This book was never about a flawless home or a minimalist ideal. It was about *freedom*. The kind that allows you to live in a way that feels honest, supportive, and aligned with who you are right now— not who you used to be, or who the world tells you to be.

Whenever you feel things creeping back in—whether it's physical clutter, emotional weight, or schedule overwhelm—remember, the tools you need are right here:

- A five-minute brain dump when your mind feels noisy

- A one-minute reset when the surface is chaotic

- A simple evening tidy to calm your environment

- A "not-to-do" list to protect your peace

- A memory box to hold what matters—and release what doesn't

- A gentle weekly review to return to clarity

- And the 21-Day Reset Challenge whenever you need a fresh start

These tools aren't just actions—they're anchors. Quiet reminders that no matter how busy life gets, **you can always choose clarity again**.

You've learned that space isn't empty. It's powerful. It gives you room to rest. To breathe. To grow. It allows your life to expand, not with more stuff—but with more meaning.

And perhaps most importantly: you've proven to yourself that you are capable. You don't have to wait for the perfect weekend, the right mindset, or someone else's approval. You know how to begin. You've already done it.

So whenever you feel stuck, overwhelmed, or pulled off track, come back to this truth:

You are allowed to reset. As many times as you need.

Your clarity is just one small action away.

Thank you for trusting me to guide you on this journey. May your home reflect your values. May your mind feel light. And may your life be filled with only what matters most.

With warmth and encouragement,
Amelia Walsh

Bonus Resources

Support for Staying Clear, Calm, and Clutter-Free

Your journey doesn't end here. Below are some tools and ideas to help you keep momentum and continue living with less—and loving it.

1. The Reset Ritual Library

Return to the reset rituals at the end of each chapter whenever you feel stuck, rushed, or overwhelmed. Keep a journal or note in your planner where you record:

- What you released

- How it made you feel

- One sentence of intention going forward

You'll start to see patterns, progress, and personal preferences that support your unique lifestyle.

2. Your Weekly Reset Plan

Choose one time each week—Sunday evening or Monday morning works well—for a 15-minute check-in. Ask yourself:

- What areas feel cluttered again?

- What one action would feel supportive this week?

- Is anything on my calendar I can cancel, delegate, or delay?

Add a gentle tidy-up, a fridge sweep, or a quick zone reset. This ritual will help you stay on top of things before they spiral.

3. Decluttering "Go-To" List

Keep a running list of small spaces you can reset in under 10 minutes. Post it inside a cupboard door or keep it on your phone.

Ideas include:

- One drawer
- Your desktop
- Under the sink
- A single shelf
- Your wallet
- Your phone's camera roll

When you want to feel accomplished quickly, go here first.

4. The Clutter Personality Quiz (Chapter 2)

Revisit your type as you grow. You may start as a *Sentimental Saver*, but over time your habits may evolve. Understanding how you relate to clutter helps you choose systems that actually work for you.

5. 21-Day Reset Challenge

Re-do the challenge as often as needed—seasonally, after a house move, when life feels messy again, or before the new year. You can also:

- Invite a friend to do it with you
- Print it and tick off each day
- Create your own version using your personal reset needs

6. Create a Reset Basket

Fill a small basket or tote with items that support your reset routine:

- Microfibre cloths
- Mini bin bags

- Post-it notes

- Pen and notepad

- Donation tags or labels

- Your journal

Keep it in an easy-to-access place so you can jump into a mini reset when the mood strikes.

7. Stay Connected to Your Why

Write your reason for decluttering on a card and keep it in your wallet, your mirror, or your bedside drawer.

Examples:

- "I want to model calm for my children."

- "I want to feel less overwhelmed when I walk through the door."

- "I want space to breathe, think, and be creative."

Revisit this whenever motivation dips. It's your personal compass.

Checklist

Your Quick Reference Guide for a Clutter-Free Life

Tick off items as you go, or keep a printed version on your fridge or inside a cupboard door.

Daily Mini-Resets

- Tidy one surface
- One-minute item return (put away immediately)
- Clear a digital notification
- Wipe a small area (sink, table, mirror)
- Journal one thought or feeling

Weekly Reset Plan

- Fridge clear-out
- Bag or car tidy
- Laundry check (clothes you didn't wear)
- Calendar review: Cancel or simplify
- Restock donation bag or box

Monthly Tasks

- Review a wardrobe section
- Let go of one sentimental item
- Clear 10 photos from phone or laptop
- Declutter one category: books, tech, craft, paper
- Share your progress with someone you trust

Mind + Schedule

- Write a "Not-To-Do" list

- Say no to one new commitment

- Schedule one day/evening of true rest

- Practice a 5-minute brain dump

- Revisit your Reset Rituals

When Things Feel Cluttered Again

- Start with a drawer or corner

- Pick any chapter and reread the Reset Ritual

- Return to the 21-Day Challenge

- Ask: What do I need *less* of right now?

- Begin again, gently

Reminder: You are never behind. Clarity is just one small action away.

Printed in Dunstable, United Kingdom

66580294R00057